I Pooped In The Potty Today

Copyright 2021 by SloboBro Ltd

I Pooped In The Potty Today

By Dillan Slobodian

For Tanya, Xayden, Adley and Zakkai as well as anyone else going through the exciting process of potty training. Potty training can be a fun, exciting, stressful and frustrating time for everyone involved. We found that emphasizing the exciting and fun parts for the kids made it a much more enjoyable and successful experience. Books and stories can really help kids look forward to potty training and want to get out of their diapers and onto the potty.

That's what this book is all about. We hope that this book will make potty training enjoyable and fun for the whole family. It will also help to remind both kids and parents that accidents happen and that is okay and to be expected, but we can't let that discourage us. We just have to get right back on that potty and try again.

Wishing you all the best on this amazing journey that is raising kids and/or growing up.

let me tell you a story all about me

And how I learned where to poop and pee

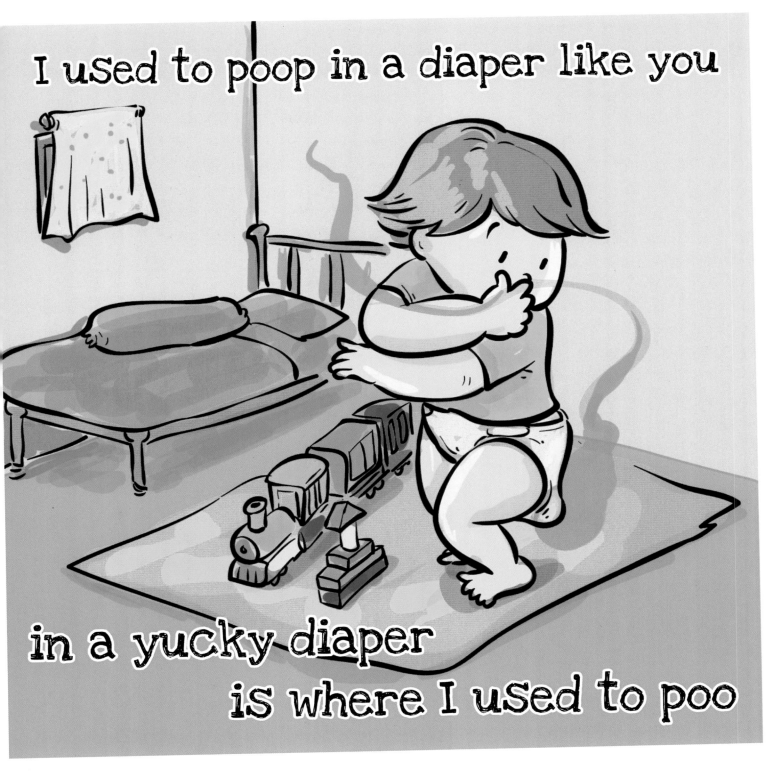

Now i'm a big kid and I use underwear

How did I get here? please let me share

I started by spending a little time nude

Or sitting on my potty while eating my food

Sometimes I had accidents and thats okay

I just got back on the potty to try again right away

Then there was the time
I pooped on the floor

Next time I pooped
on the potty like
I did before

I couldn't always make it in time

but I didn't give up because I knew it'd be fine

BECAUSE NOW...

To poop in the potty is much cleaner for you

So I go to the potty

when I have to poo

Now I poop in the potty without a care.

I no longer have accidents
and I wear underwear